Mel Bay Presents

Best of COUNTRY GUITAR SOLOS

By Tommy Flint

DEDICATION

To June Thompson and Paul George
Two caring, loving, spiritually beautiful and very wise people,
Who taught me that in life I have the right to make choices—
And to love and respect myself as well as others.
Thanks for caring.

Tommy Flint

Contents

Walking with the Blues

Tommy Flint

3

The Skaters
(Les Patineurs)

WALDTEUFEL
Arr. by Tommy Flint

Expressive medium waltz

4

Rainy Night Blues

Fisher's Hornpipe

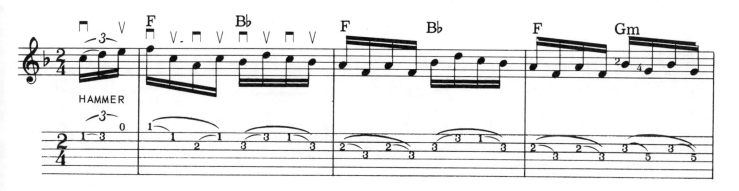

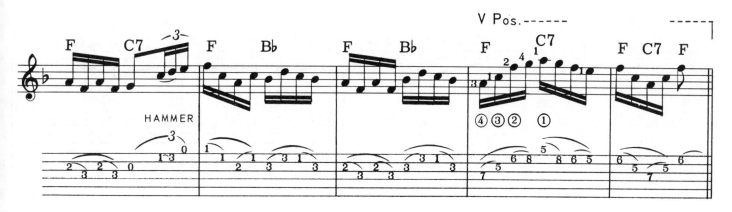

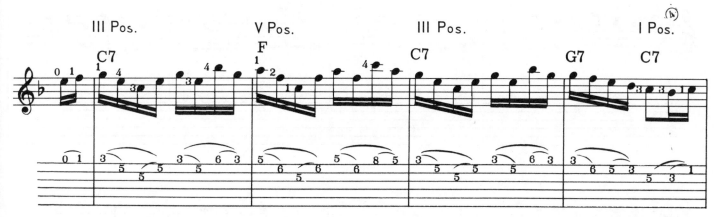

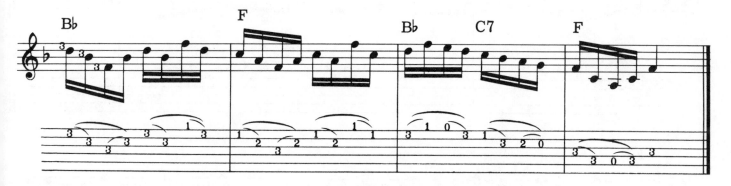

RHYTHM CHORDS FOR FISHER'S HORNPIPE

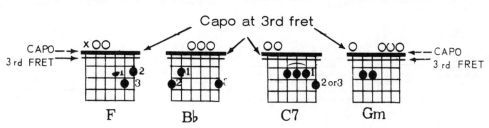

Rocking the Pick

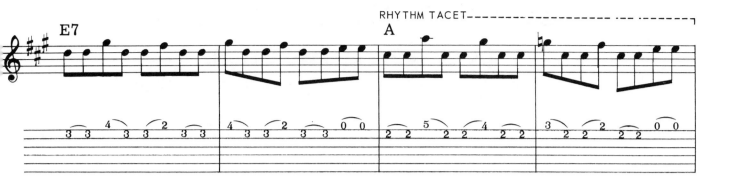

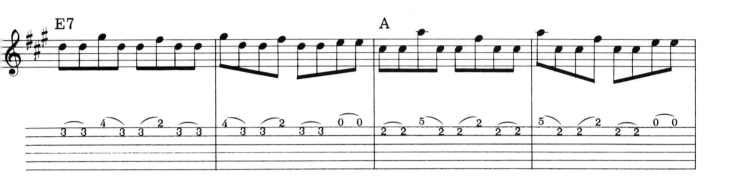

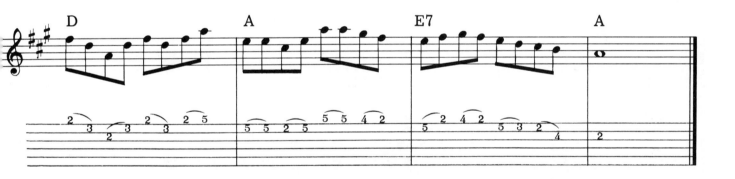

Some flat pickers feel that more speed may be obtained
by using this method of picking.

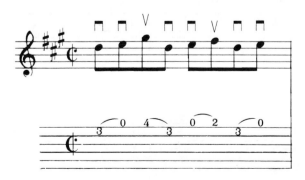

Heliotrope Bouquet
(A Slow Drag Two-Step)

By Louis Chauvin
&
By SCOTT JOPLIN
Arr. by TOMMY FLINT

Liberty

This melody is based on a combination of the chordal and scale tones.

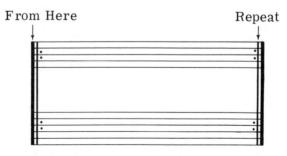

Fannie Lou

TOMMY FLINT

Rough River Hoedown

TOMMY FLINT

Company Store Boogie

TOMMY FLINT

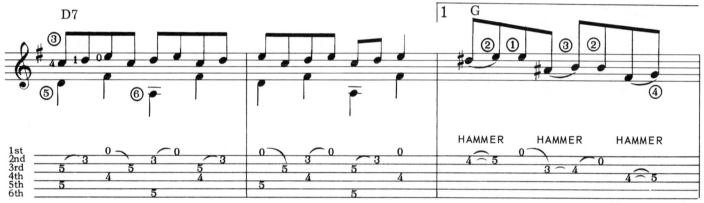

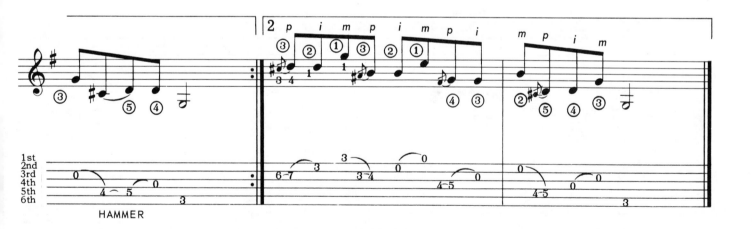

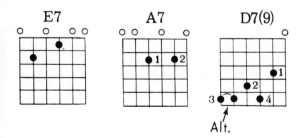

HOLD CHORDS, USE FOURTH FINGER TO PLAY NOTES ON THE
FOURTH FRET ON BASS LINE. (G#, C#, F#)

Old Joe Clark

Bill Cheatham

The slurs are optional. All notes may be picked if you wish. Use alternate picking.

TWANGING SERENADE

SWINGING COUNTRY SHUFFLE

INTRO			
G	G	C	C G G G
V1			
C	C	F	F
D	D	G	G
C	C	F	F
G	G	C	C G G G
V2			
C	C	F	F
D	D	G	G
C	C	F	F
G	G	C	C
B1			
G	G	C	C
D	D	G	G
C	C	F	F
G	G	C	C
B2			
F	C	G	C
V3			
C	C	F	F
D	D	G	G
C	C	F	F
G	G	C	C
OUTRO			
G	G	C	C

Steel Serenade

SHUFFLE RHYTHM

TOMMY FLINT

John Henry

Soldier's Joy

"TAG" ENDING FOR SOLDIER'S JOY

The Country Boy Shuffle

TOMMY FLINT

Billy in the Lowground

THE CHORUS CAN BE PLAYED AN OCTAVE HIGHER

etc.

Under the Double Eagle

Amazing Grace

When playing in $\frac{3}{4}$ or waltz time the thumb and index finger are frequently used together in playing the rhythm strokes. In measure number one of the following solo the thumb and middle finger are used on the first beat. The thumb and index finger are used to play the rhythm stroke on the second beat. The middle and index fingers are used for the eighth notes on the third beat.

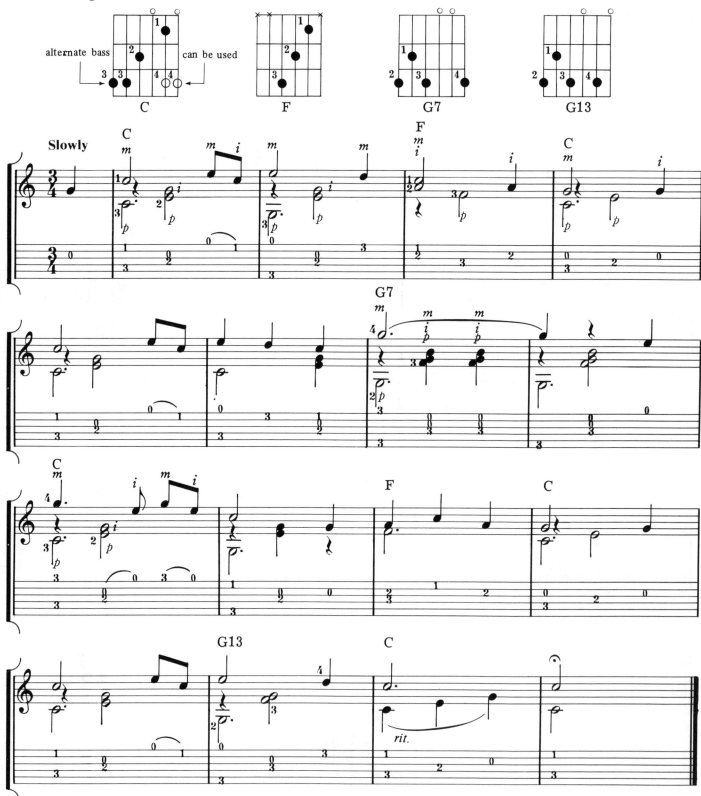

Leather Britches

Most fiddlers play this in the key of G. This arrangement is very easy to transpose to G by placing a capo on the seventh fret. Use the same fingering.

Brightly

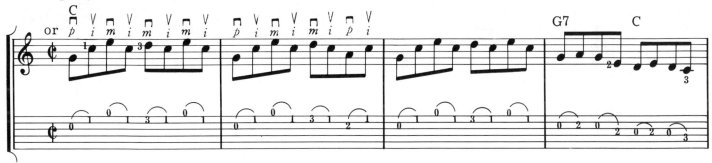

THE CHORUS CAN BE PLAYED AN OCTAVE HIGHER IN THE KEY OF C.

Example

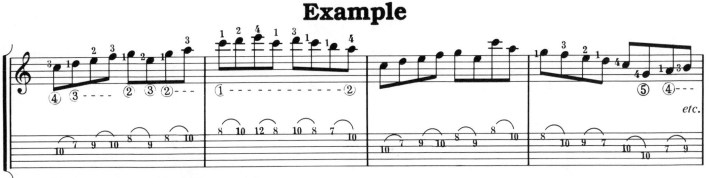

Slurs can be omitted if you wish.

Irish Washwoman

Muhlenberg County Blues

TOMMY FLINT

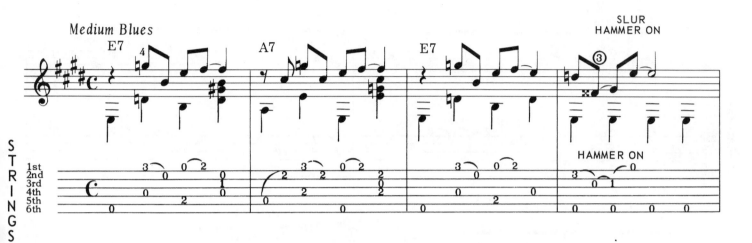

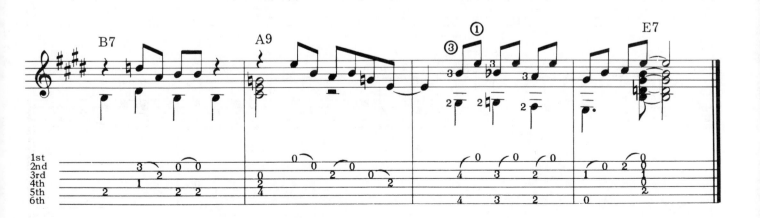

Southern Bound

The open (1) string can be used with all chords on this page

Fire on the Mountain

Pacific to Green Bay
(A Tribute to Bill and Mel Bay)

Tommy Flint

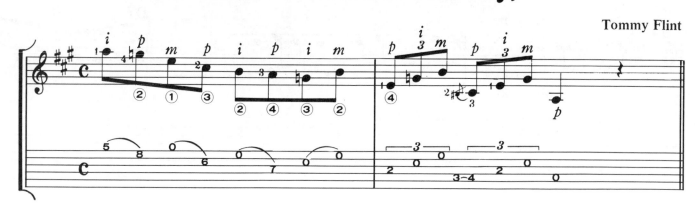

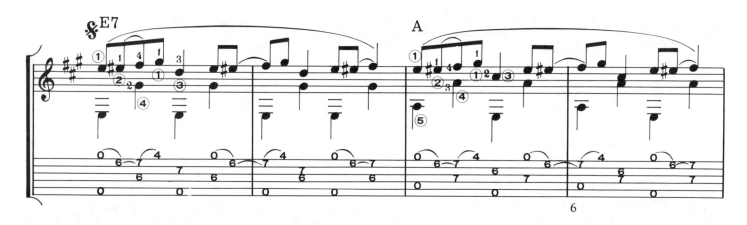

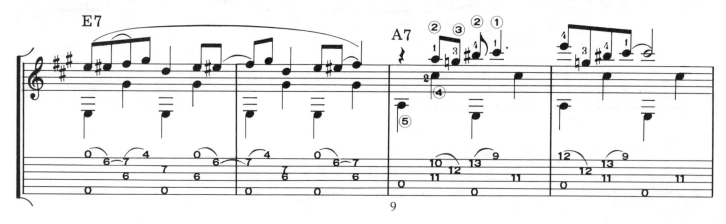

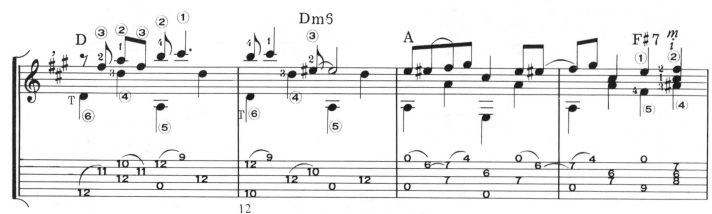

Chords Used in
Pacific to Green Bay

E7
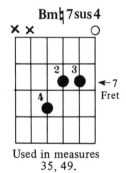
Used in measures
3,4,7,8,19,20,23,
24,31,32,67,68,95,
96,101,102,105,106
109,110.

A
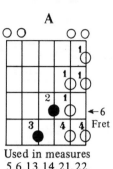
Used in measures
5,6,13,14,21,22,
29,30,37,38,54,69,
70,77,78,85,86,93,
94,99,100,103,104.

A7(9)
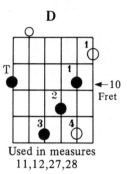
Used in measures
9,10,25,26,41,42
57,58,73,74,89,90.

D
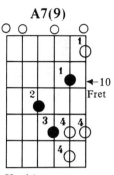
Used in measures
11,12,27,28

Dm6
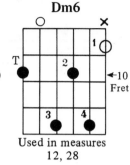
Used in measures
12, 28

B7
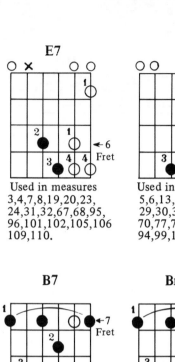
Used in measures
15, 16, 48, 79, 80
½ barre

Bm7
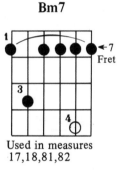
Used in measures
17,18,81,82

E7
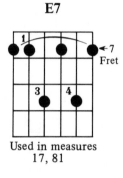
Used in measures
17, 81

E7♭9
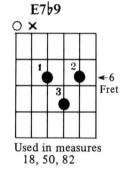
Used in measures
18, 50, 82

Bmsus4
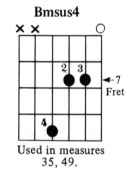
Used in measures
35, 49.

Bm♮7sus4
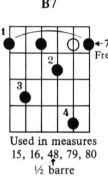
Used in measures
35, 49.

Bm7sus4
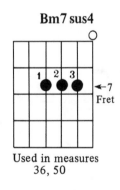
Used in measures
36, 50

E9
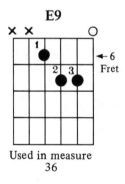
Used in measure
36

Aadd9
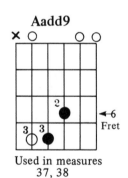
Used in measures
37, 38

A Maj. 9
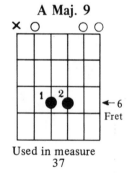
Used in measure
37

A 9/6
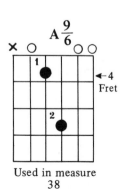
Used in measure
38

E9
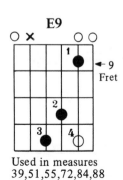
Used in measures
39,51,55,72,84,88

E13
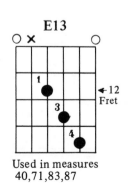
Used in measures
40,71,83,87

D6
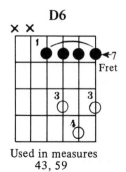
Used in measures
43, 59

Dm6
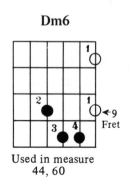
Used in measure
44, 60

Chords Used in
Pacific to Green Bay

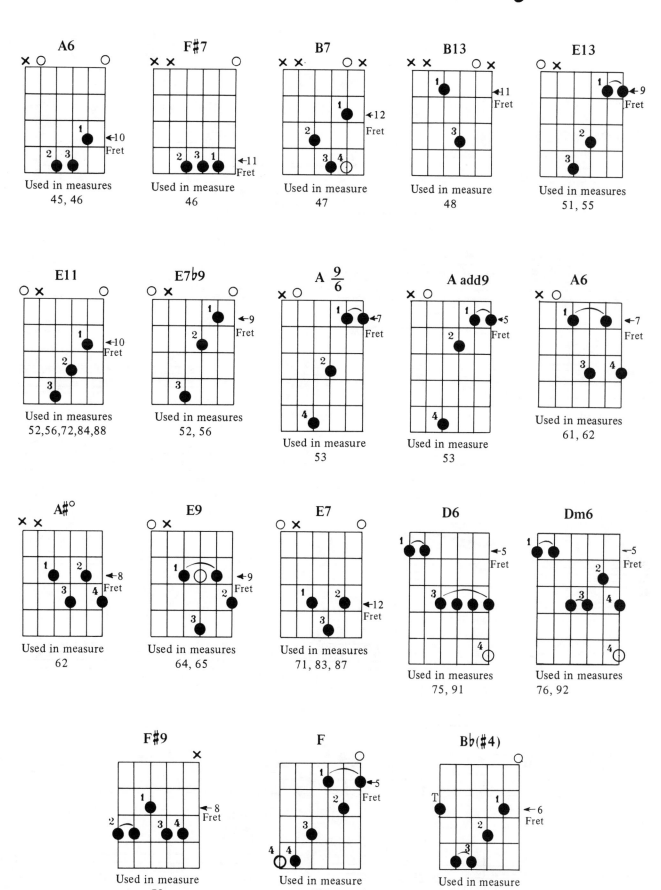

The Tennessee Steel

TOMMY FLINT

Blues for Mose

TOMMY FLINT

A Triplet Run

Space all notes evenly.

Turkey in the Straw

Lonesome Road Blues

Spanish Fandango

Moderately bright

Traditional

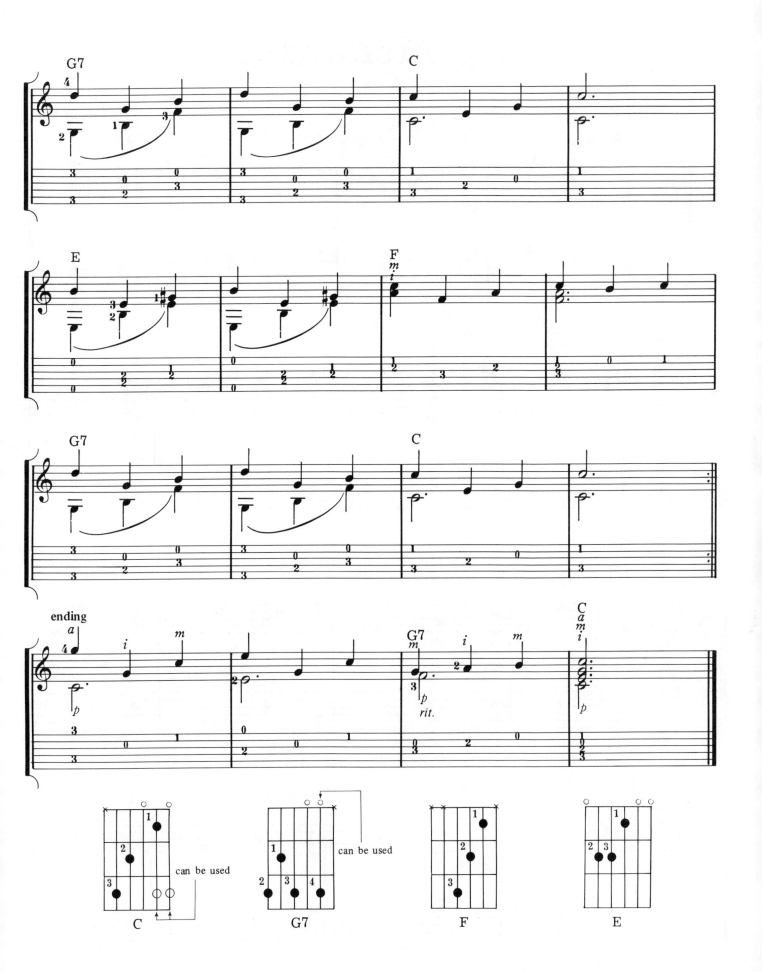

My Memories

Tommy Flint

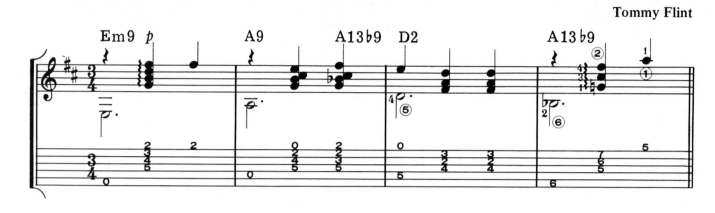

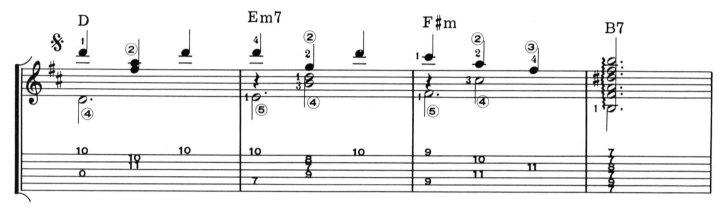

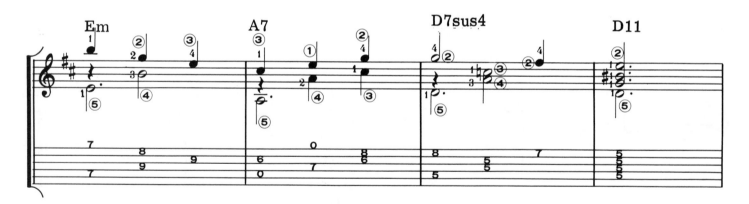

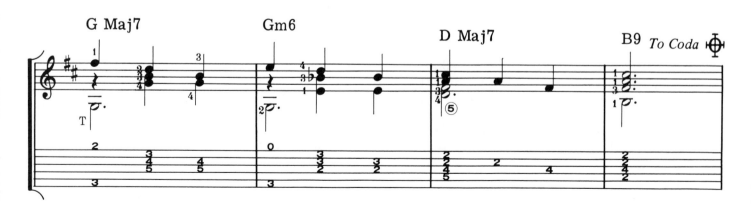

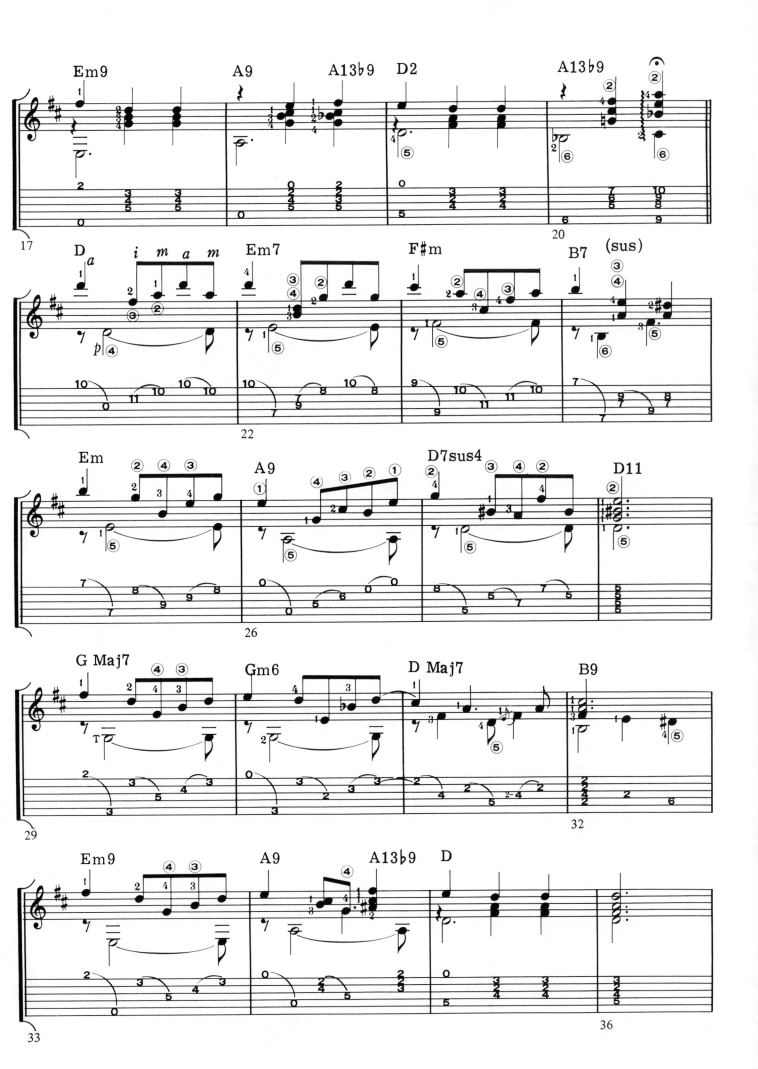

* Use index Finger of right hand to depress "B" note on ⑥ string. Use thumb (*p*) to pluck the strings.

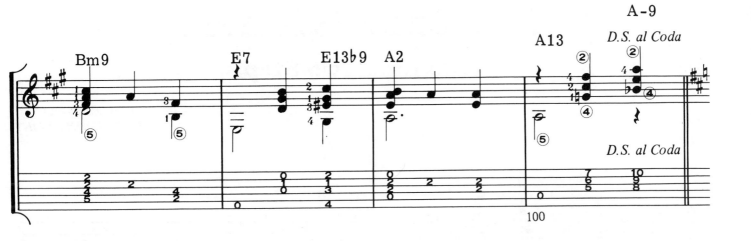

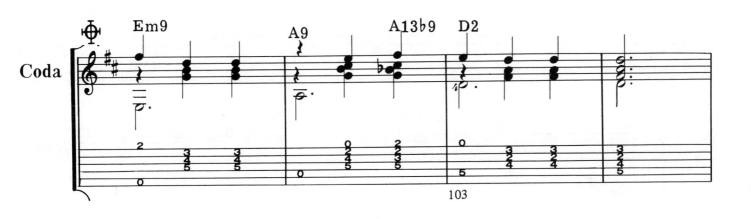

Coda

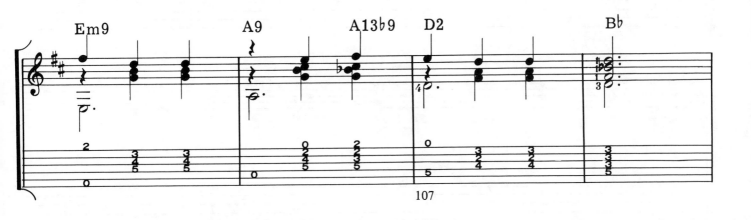

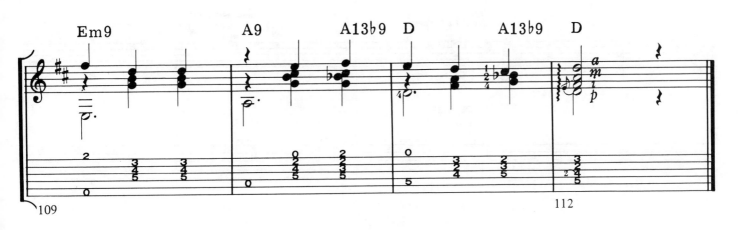

The Easy Winners
(A Ragtime Two-Step)

By SCOTT JOPLIN
Arr. by TOMMY FLINT

54

Movin' On